Take a Gap Year

Emma Parahus

Dedications

To my family and friends,

Who have always supported me

And to me,

Because I need some credit

Contents

Introduction

I was nearly 18 when I wanted to seek something bigger, something worthwhile. I found myself a little lost, almost out of place. Time stood still, and days passed like years. I knew this wasn't who I was; or who I wanted to become. After some research, I discovered a 25-week travel program designed to discover myself and the world.

I courageously took the path less traveled and never looked back. It completely altered my perspective on the world and, most importantly, life itself. Traveling taught me to live simpler, love harder, and make the most out of my time. Once I realized that, my life started to begin.

Chapter 1

The Alternate Path

The room was dimly-lit. I was in (what would I call) 'sad pajamas.' On my bed were empty Lay's wrappers, and I could see at least two empty soda cans on the floor. It was one of those days, you know? Where you want to stay on your bed, losing track of time and wondering what is going on. I don't want to use the word depression, but I was beginning to think I was at least close to that point.

I wanted to get out of bed and make myself a coffee. I gathered energy for a few seconds but then was unable to. Why do I feel as if I was a century-old woman who might as well be dead?! I was still not an adult; I was merely a teenager. Yet, I felt as if I had been alive for ages.

"What is the meaning of all this?" I whispered into the darkness, hoping for a divine voice to tell me what I needed to hear. But there was nothing but silence.

What were we all here for? Are we not supposed to live our lives as we like? Are we supposed to surrender to whatever society thinks of us? Fall prey to traditions that hinder our growth as people?

What was wrong with me? Why did I have this darkness inside me? An emptiness. I was itching for something bigger. I felt as if I didn't fill this void; it would consume me. I was only 17, and some would say I was too much of a pessimist, but isn't it a good thing that I am thinking of all this? Being aware of what's going on and actually asking questions that matter.

What is with the people around you, anyway? At 17, everyone expects you to know what you want to do for the rest of your days.

What is your major in college? Where do you see yourself in five years? Have you thought about getting additional degrees? Where do you plan to settle? Okay, give me a break.

Let me elaborate on my point. I never understood how we were supposed to have it all figured out. I mean, I have seen adults who have nothing figured out, but they can get away with things only because they are adults.

Oh, please. The hypocrisy is literally in front of you. We aren't even allowed to vote, and they are expecting us to already chart a successful life.

I finally got out of bed with a loud grunt. I was tired of everything, but I felt thirsty. I walked over to the table, poured myself a glass of water from the jug, and drank it in one go.

I didn't realize how thirsty I had been till I had. I poured myself another glass of water and went back to bed. I sat there and looked out the window.

Isn't it amazing how everyone goes through life without caring about the things that should matter? This normal life that people seek ends up overshadowing everything else. Get to a respected university so that you get a good job.

Yes, let's think about that. Ensuring that you do well enough in all the courses reflects on your overall score. Yes, an important concern. But do they stop and think about what is happening while they fret over such things? Look at climate change. The earth is dying a slow death. People are getting their whole lives destroyed due to floods. There are homeless people unable to eat something, while others waste food just like that.

Kids go to school in the morning, only to get shot and return dead to their homes. I know I am only 17, but even I can see that it's not just me who is struggling. Things aren't okay with the world, and the world itself has a void that people don't realize or just simply ignore. For me, this race towards better universities isn't just it. There has to be something bigger. Something more.

I remember my school days; that was the time when I started realizing how tired I was of this monotonous race of life. I grew up in a small town and attended a private catholic school. I was part of a big family, and I never had any complaints. I had everything.

But then, what about those who have nothing? Or, what if I had nothing? Would I be able to survive or perish? This is something that has been bugging me for a while now.

I thought about those who are born in dark alleys and downtrodden houses. These people have nothing. Then, I look at myself. I have had everything in the world. No, I am not being ungrateful. In fact, I have been blessed in so many aspects. I have had family who had my back and friends I could always count on. But then, will I ever be able to know more or feel more if I am forever stuck to where I have been? What would I have to my own name when I think about it later on in my life?

I have decided I will not settle for this kind of life. But little did I know that in the next few days, fate would weave its magic wand. It took me about 3 weeks to find it, but eventually, I did.

I spent sleepless nights researching and searching for it. I remember hopping from one website to another till I came across the perfect thing. It was one of those "Tada!" moments. It was just what I needed. The 25-week gap year program was designed to discover yourself and the world.

Was it going to be as awesome as it sounds? I had no clue back then. But it was a program that I hoped would ignite my desire to see what the world has to offer.

Later that night, I had a dream. I was in a place where there was nothing. No, really. Nothing. It was an empty space. I remember feeling confused, an emotion I felt all too much in recent times. It was then that I saw a bright light right in front of me. I felt this warmth, and I decided to follow it. As soon as I entered the light, I woke up. I had nothing but one thought. I need to get into this program. This was it. This was what I needed.

But I was scared to introduce this idea to my parents. I feared they would dismiss the whole idea. They would think it's nothing but a waste of time. I didn't want them to say no, and thankfully they didn't. In fact, they encouraged me to go for it. They were happy that I felt it was important.

I hoped that my friends understood this too, but they were confused more than anything. But I knew what I was doing. I was confident, pumped up, and for the first time, perhaps, I felt I was going to break free from this rut. I also decided I won't let anything cloud my judgment.

It was the first time I was going on a trip like this. The plan was to meet my cohort in Boston. But I didn't know what to pack and how to pack it. My mom gladly helped me. Once we were done, it was time for goodbyes. Realizing that I won't be seeing my best friends for a long time was difficult. I knew I would miss them tremendously, but I knew I had to do this on my own. This was my thing, and I needed to own it. I remember reading a story about how a butterfly has to break open its own cocoon to get free.

If someone else does it for them, they die. The butterfly needed to get uncomfortable to be comfortable again. These friends have been with me from the very beginning, but it was time to see what else the world has for me. It was time to meet people from different backgrounds to make new, hopefully long-lasting friendships.

Due to certain reasons, I was going to be late. Even though I had hurried as much as possible, I was still new to this. I said bye to my parents and hopped on my assigned bus to head to dinner. The people on the bus would be the ones I'd be spending a year with.

The most amazing, gentle, kindest people I've ever met. But did I know it back then? No. I was anxious about it all, so I just found my seat and sat there quietly. I talked to the girl who was next to me. I was nervous, and I couldn't talk much. She told me she lived in Ohio, and she rushed here as well.

I remember thinking if I made a mistake. It was going to be a long time. What the hell did I just walk into? I was shivering. But I wasn't the only one. I noticed how other people on the bus felt anxious, too. Some more than others. But I took a deep breath and felt proud of myself. What I was doing was difficult, and yet I was there, doing it. Now, all I needed was to find my people, and everything will be okay. I think the collective understanding that we were all in this together made it easier.

The place we were staying was a facility that was quite spacious. After the first day, I settled in. Food helped! They had made amazing food for us, and it calmed down my nerves. I was even able to have small talk with another girl.

I realized that I had never met anyone like these people. Some were extroverted; they were regularly talking with other people, while some seemed shy. Some were too loud and honestly annoying. But I felt all shared a spark. A spark that I felt in myself too.

Like the light that I had seen in my dream. Everyone was so unapologetically themselves. I honestly felt I could like it here. These people cared about you, and I was beginning to care for them. It felt like a bond was being made without any of us truly realizing it.

There was an air of empathy, a sense of belonging. I knew I was going to see so much with them and experience things that would change our lives. We spent most of our time bouncing back and forth between our hotel and the EF Headquarters. I found out that there were 80 students in total.

We were given an orientation session at the headquarters. We talked about traveling safety, goals, itinerary, and so much more. After that, we were all assigned counselors who would help us further.

Mine was Miss Kennedy. She told me how I'd get support every step of the way. She instructed me that the most important resource that we all have is time. How can this one single thing make or break our lives?

She reminded me that I was at the perfect time in my life to discover who I am. Even though I was quiet outside, listening to her inside, I felt so excited. It reaffirmed my faith that I was doing the right thing. Miss Kennedy told me that this program is not an alternative to college.

However, it's there to make me feel ready and make the most of my academic future and the rest of my life. It will help me see the world, and learn about new cultures languages, and meet people.

We were greeted by other advisors and alumni too, who had interesting stories to share. We were even told to write a letter to our future selves, which would be opened in London, on the last day of the program. Here's what I wrote:

Take a leap of faith. I hope this year was everything you ever dreamed of; I am so proud of you.

We got ready for the next step and were given further instructions by advisors. Finally, we were told to 'conquer the world.'

We all took off on our flight to Europe. It was a night flight. I sat next to this kid, Jake. Maybe I met him once during orientation; he had sandwiches. But I didn't know anything about him.

I didn't realize it, but I ended up falling asleep literally on top of him, and he was nice about it. He only woke me up for dinner.

I was apologetic, but he said it was okay. In a very interesting way, I made an acquaintance in the strangest of circumstances. After having dinner, I slept again. The flight took over 7 hours. When it landed, it felt amazing. I was thousands of miles away in Paris.

Chapter 2

Living Abroad

My first stop was Paris; we all spent the next two weeks backpacking around Europe. *I* had never seen a European city before. So, this was just like watching a film or reading a book. I didn't know how much travel experience other students had, but I am sure it was breathtaking for all 80 of us. We were separated, however, so we all had a different, quite personal experience.

Being in so many different places was quite overwhelming. I felt physically tired, but I still loved every moment. It was one of those things, you know? The experience is exhausting, and yet it leaves you with so much fulfillment. It literally felt like I was dreaming.

I was always in a state of disbelief. Was this real? I was always so tired at the end of the day; I used all my energy to stay in the present. I didn't want to miss a single moment.

There are those times when you want to sit under the sun and soak up every ray of sunlight during winter. This was precisely how I felt. I soaked up every moment, and honestly, I strayed away from the group a lot of times because I wanted to experience everything on my own. Being in solitude. But I was also bonding with the group in my own way. We all started to get close, and I was beginning to feel comfortable around everyone.

We all were in awe of the world; it was hard to grasp. After those 2 weeks in the city, we all were off to the destination we chose for language study. My choice was Barcelona, along with 20 other people. The city fascinated me while I was researching, and frankly, I wanted to experience it firsthand.

The program's management had arranged for us to stay as guests with different families. I arrived at my family's house and saw that it was a tiny apartment. How would I fit in it? I dragged my luggage and looked around. Out of nowhere, a little girl ran to me, latching onto my leg. She looked the same age as my niece.

My host mom, who was quite welcoming, led me to my tiny room, where I'd be staying for the next 6 weeks. The room was perfect, and I would definitely fit in it! It felt warm and cozy. I kept my luggage in the room and sat on the bed. It felt very comfortable. Now that I think of it, it is a huge thing to feel comfortable in a house you aren't familiar with. So, I was really grateful.

I was looking around the room; it had a light pink color and was clean. I saw the little girl, who had been latching on my leg, entering the room. Her name, as I had learned, was Julia. She was three years old. We didn't speak the same language, but there was this mutual connection.

I think it all comes down to us just being humans. Somehow, we can make a connection with someone from an entirely different culture who speaks a different language. I had been worried that the language barrier might be a bit too much for me, but this feeling of being able to understand her calmed me down.

I realized then that it wouldn't be hard to communicate with her. Whether it was dancing to her favorite songs, watching her favorite cartoons, or just laughing together, we bonded during every single moment. We had become friends.

Her older sister, Antuantte, was most fluent in English. So, for all the things that I couldn't understand, she helped me. I had found my host family to be so affectionate. They were always kind to me and ensured that I was cared for. It calmed my anxiety to a point where I felt truly relaxed.

My host mom, dad, and two sisters spent the first night getting to know me. They saw me as more than a "spoiled American girl." In fact, I felt they were as excited to have me as I was to be there! They discussed what I was passionate about, my hobbies, my family, my friends there, and everything else.

I must admit it was a bit difficult for me to find my way around the language barrier at first. But that's where technology came to my aid. Google Translate was a lifesaver! As I talked, I started getting acquainted with their language, and it made me feel lucky to be a part of this. I felt loved.

I remember thinking how crazy it was that despite having a small apartment, they had such big hearts to welcome me. I was worried it wouldn't be comfortable. How silly of me! It turned out to be more than comfortable- it was home.

I thought back to my house in New York and realized that the size of my kitchen was probably the size of their whole apartment! Yet, they were absolutely content with it. But I kept thinking, how could they fit their whole life into this? Didn't it feel suffocating at times?

Then I realized that they didn't have too many material things around. They had all the essentials- a kitchen, dining room, and living room. All your basic necessities. They had each other, and that's all that mattered to them. It truly felt like home. A home away from home.

The module of my program that I was in was language study. Every day, Monday through Friday, students from all around the world got together in the comfort of the EF school to learn Spanish.

Getting to school and returning home was difficult initially because I was so new to the metro. But locals were always kind and guided me in the right direction whenever needed, in the best way they could. People here were pretty good at English, so they were always willing to give directions.

Meanwhile, at school, there were familiar faces and friends from my cohort in America, but primarily international students. There were kids from Italy, Germany, Switzerland, and the Netherlands. It was so fascinating that the program allowed me to be among people from different cultures. I was so excited to get to know everyone.

The way they talked, the way they ate, the way they engaged with other people: everything. Their values were so different from the United States- I wanted to be just like them; I was honestly kind of jealous of how they were raised.

Back home, things weren't like that. These people were understanding, generous, and caring. I thought- How did America become the way that it is, so cruel and separated when this is how other countries lived?

In one of my first classes, I made a friend named Tara. She lived in Amsterdam. I told her how much I loved this coffee shop down the street. Didn't think much of it- just small talk. The next day, she comes in with an iced coffee for me. The same iced coffee I told her about yesterday. Who does that?

These people! It warmed my heart so much and made me want to be as giving as her. Each day, I kind of felt myself forming as a person. Becoming more like them. I loved spending time with them; they made me feel so loved. Underneath all of our differences, all of us somehow shared the same passion for searching for something bigger in the world.

They were so wise with cultural awareness. I admired them so much. I honestly felt so stupid talking to them since I was caught up in what I felt was like a well, like a frog stuck in a well, unable to see what was outside. This was American life for me. These kids had experienced so much; they had explored things that we, as American students, had no idea about.

On the other hand, I had fallen in love with Barcelona. The city was beautiful, and the architecture was outstanding. There was so much history, and I could see well-preserved heritage at every corner. I just hadn't fallen in love with the city that was out there, the physical city. I had also grown fond of the people.

The compassion and love they gave people were indescribable. It didn't matter who you were. You could be from anywhere in the world; they would welcome you with a warm embrace. They would go out of their way to make you feel comfortable. Americans would never do that, trust me.

These people lived freely, with a sense of fulfillment and passion. They even took 2 hours out of their workday to go home, eat lunch, nap, and spend time with their family. Also, the food! I wish I could describe how amazing the food was! I can't even begin to describe the difference in food culture between Europe and America.

My family would cook dinner every night, and we all talked about our day while eating amazing, fresh food. Nothing came out of cans.

None of that frozen food. No fried chicken sandwiches that always tasted the same or oily french fries. There were always beautifully green salads, farm-fresh boiled eggs, pure organic chicken, and much more. I never got sick once. My stomach was never bloated, and my body never felt better. Even my mental state was so pure-everything stemmed from refined food. No corn syrup, added artificial flavors, nothing.

I remember one night at dinner. Antuantte asked me about the president of the United States, Joe Biden. They were all making jokes, so I joined in too. They were saying how funny all the political drama in America is.

After we talked about it, I was curious about their president. And I swear to you, Antuantte looked at me and said, "I have no idea," using her English words in her Spanish accent. I was like, "What?" How did she *not* know her government but know everything about mine? It told me a lot about how America is a joke to the people here.

For 6 weeks, I truly lived a life I had never dreamt of. I saw everything the city had to offer; even my parents came to visit. I showed them around; I got so embarrassed since they acted so "American." Even though I would do the same thing 6 weeks ago, it all had changed for me. The experience has given me so much.

But now, my time in the city was coming to an end. Saying goodbye to a place where I felt utterly at peace was going to be difficult. The realization that I would never live with my host family again was hard. I felt like I had left a part of me there. But I had to go.

Six weeks were over, and I needed to start the next 6 weeks in Costa Rica, doing community service. I was so excited for the next module but also sad because I was leaving behind the love of my life: Barcelona.

Chapter 3

Mary

I was never really that strong in my faith. I went to Catholic school and went to Church whenever I was told. I always tried to do the right thing. The "Godly" thing. But it never really clicked with me fully, you know, God? The idea of God felt so forced and repetitive. At least the ritualistic aspect of it. So, you sit down for Church, you stand up, you sit down, and you wait for it to be over.

Do you understand what I mean? It honestly felt like nobody was really present; nobody was truly focused... including me. But it all changed when I met her.

All the dots connected, and everything clicked when I met Mary. She was a girl from Georgia, just another peer in my cohort and one of the 20 students who chose Barcelona. My best friend, my rock. But I didn't know at the time that this Mary would become *my* Mary. I didn't know it until Barcelona.

I had never really met anybody like her. She was trailed by a ray of sunlight like an angel. I know you might say I am exaggerating, but trust me, she was unbelievable. The most soft-spoken but most powerful girl I've ever met.

She carried herself with such grace that you almost felt like you were communicating with God himself. She was my connection to Him. I've always believed in God, but after having some tough times in high school, I felt as if he had betrayed me; left me alone.

She, somehow, brought me back to Him. Not just because she was so strong in her faith but because she put words into actions. She lived the word of God every day. I could see it.

Little by little, *I* started doing the same things. Buying flowers for strangers, going to Church willingly, and waking up every day with gratitude. Dictating my life and acknowledging what's really important allowed me to see a different side of myself. A side of myself that I was so proud of. A side of me that would never have opened if I never took a gap year. It really changed everything for me.

She changed everything for me. How I looked at life, and most importantly, how I looked at people. She taught me that everyone has a story and everyone has something going on. She believed that there was good in everyone, and she gave everyone a chance.

And even if she was betrayed, she always forgave. I don't know how she did that, but I wanted to find out. She was just another peer in my cohort, a girl from Georgia. How was she everything I ever needed? It's astonishing. But her energy was so powerful it felt like everybody was trying to drift towards her.

We talked a couple of times in Boston, but I didn't really know much about her besides that she was different. I later found out that she was unbelievably different in the perfect way. She didn't care about drinking, partying, vaping, or everything else like that. She used her time in different ways. To improve herself in ways that would set herself apart from so many people of my age.

From reading self-help books or just talking about her dreams that she was so passionate about, Mary was someone that you just knew would succeed in life; you could tell that just by looking at her. Those people just get it.

The people who want to escape the 9-5 work-life mentality and make their lives mean something. Anything she ever wanted in life, she got. Because she believed it was attainable. Anything was within arm's reach.

She thought 5 times more than everyone else. She wasn't necessarily smarter; she just could think bigger than most people. Honestly, most people don't think. They believe the traditions of 40 years ago are still valid today.

For example, why do some people still believe that women aren't equal to men? Or, why do people refuse to see that the American system of 'grinding' at work is actually harmful to us all?

They think everything should stay the same, even when our world is crumbling apart. People don't think outside the box. They become too 'comfortable' with how things are.

Who likes change? No one. So, we fall prey to what society tells us and don't try to think bigger. To think maybe, just maybe, I can get out of this hamster wheel of life. Working hard at the expense of your mental well-being should not be an indicator of your success.

That happiness isn't just standing in endless lines on Black Friday. So, take a deep breath and think. What *does* America want? What is the American Dream really about? Just … work and work and work, without stopping for a moment. They have practically been training us since we were 5 years old to listen to somebody else and not ourselves.

Just think of this for a moment. As a kid, you're listening to your teachers. In high school, you're listening to your football coach. In college, you're listening to your professors to ensure you get this degree, even though you are clueless about what it entitles you to.

But you *have* to get it, right? Everyone else is doing it. Frankly, most people are falling into that trap. I knew then that this was my person. The missing link that I've been looking for. I thought I was going to find my people, but I found my person.

As I mentioned earlier, we had both chosen Barcelona for our language study module, so that's where we got close. We had been friendly in Boston and the next two weeks backpacking around Europe. But not like Barcelona. It's kind of funny how we first became close. We had just been dropped off in the van at our host family's house. After talking with my host family, I started walking around to find the local shops and restaurants. I needed to find good local spots since I was going to be living here for the next six weeks.

Picture this: I am walking when I hear someone scream my name from a highly elevated surface. Guess who it was? It was Mary!

She was waving her hands like a lunatic to try to catch my attention. We weren't even that close, but she always had that welcoming vibe to her. You know, those kinds of people that you just feel comfortable around? That you could open your heart to?

She made you feel like you belonged. I met her host mom, who almost immediately became like a second mom to me. That day was one of the greatest days of my life, and I didn't even know it then.

The next week we went skydiving. Something I never thought I would agree to. In fact, the thought of falling 14,000 feet from the sky and praying your parachute opens never even occurred to me! When Mary mentioned the idea to me, I completely shut it down.

I was terrified! Why would I even think of something like that? Yet, somehow, the next day, we booked it.

I never knew someone could convince me to do something so fast; that was so frightening to me. But she just did. Her energy and her excitement made me push my fear aside. She had calmed me down, persuaded me, and assured me that everything would be fine. She made me realize that I needed to do something out of my comfort zone.

Skydiving fits the bill. Skydiving was *definitely* out of my comfort zone. Skydiving meant so much more to me than just falling out of a plane, and what I experienced up there was something unreal.

When the wind hit my face the second we jumped, it felt as if I had left everything behind. Not a single ounce of worry or stress. A second of pure bliss. Indescribable bliss. Seeing the whole world at your fingertips.

Everything literally felt so small, so trivial. Every problem, every challenge in your life just disappears into the air when you're up there. I was able to experience that feeling at 18 years old while all my friends were in college. I felt grateful … I felt fulfilled.

Getting to know Mary for six weeks in Barcelona created something that both of us will treasure forever. Every day we would talk about our dreams and everything we wanted to be in life.

I had never met someone like her, so I felt things I hadn't before. It was pure joy. We would laugh like no other. I could be my true, authentic self around her, and I knew she would accept me. We would miss flights, trains, and buses. We never got mad at each other; we would just laugh. These things seemed meaningless.

Like it didn't really matter that we missed our train because we could just catch the next one.

Most people would get mad at their friends for not setting their alarm and resulting in us missing our train, but we just laughed. And laughed and laughed. We both had this understanding that the world was so much bigger than drama.

Also, the idea of partying. We absolutely loved going out with our friends and meeting new people, but there was a collective understanding that this was not the life we wanted in the long run. We were more of the movie night with a bowl of popcorn kind of girls.

Was it fun to party sometimes? Of course! We went to clubs with our new international friends a lot! But to get wrapped up in the cycle of getting wasted every weekend and trying to put your life back together every week is different. I honestly feared that kind of life.

That 9-5 work life and going crazy on the weekends because that was the only freedom you had. Corporate America- the biggest scam of all time. Working until you die. And maybe getting 5 years work-free at 80, when your bones are crippling, and you can barely climb the stairs. When you travel, you'll start to understand more. I did! Life shouldn't be like this. It should be something way different.

On the weekends, we didn't have school, so it was a chance to travel to different places or just chill at home. On one of our weekend trips, we went to Venice, Italy. It was akin to a spectacular dream. Being there with my best friend made the destination even more beautiful.

We spent the first day exploring each and every inch of the city. I'm serious, every inch! It was mesmerizing because there were no cars. You get around by boat or just walking. I used to hear tales about how gorgeous the city was, and now I knew everything was even more beautiful than I had heard.

The city was vibrant. That night, we went to bed laughing and reminiscing about our day. We woke up the next morning, still tired from the day before. We started getting dressed because, as a tourist, you're "supposed" to spend every day exploring and not wasting a minute.

I was putting on my mascara when Mary looked at me and said, "Can we just stay in today?" I'm so glad she said it because I was thinking about it too. We laughed. We figured something was wrong with us because why wouldn't we want to be like normal tourists?

We spent the day in our pajamas and ordered Mcdonald's on UberEats. We couldn't believe we were eating Mcdonald's in our bed with the best food in the world just a walk down the street. But that made it even more awesome!

We were comfortable; it felt like home because we had each other. Anyways, we spent the day laughing and writing a journal entry. It was kind of messy, but it wrote:

I've realized a few things about happiness and traveling. So, the experience of traveling the world, for a lot of people, is the ultimate dream in life. "Oh, if only I could pack up my things, quit my job, and travel the world ... I would be happy." People romanticize it so much to the point where they think the grass is so much greener over here.

That "their life isn't as great because they are stuck in the same town, with the same people, with a job that doesn't pay enough" But what I realized is that the grass is greener where you water it.

Drinking champagne at the top of the Eiffel Tower after a fancy dinner, for example, is the same rush of adrenaline and happiness that you feel at home when you are driving around with your best friends.

Yes, it may be cooler to do the first, but internally, it is the same. Happiness doesn't come from *where* you are but *from how* you choose to experience every "ordinary" day.

If you choose to find joy in every day, such as loving yourself, being grateful for the little blessings, doing random acts of kindness for your friends and family, and overly freaking out about the cute flowers in the grocery store, every day can be as great as you would imagine being at the top of the Eiffel Tower would be.

Your relationship with yourself is your superpower. I am so grateful for traveling the world, meeting people from different countries, kayaking in the brightest of blue waters, and getting to see some of the most famous and beautiful sights in the world. It is truly the best thing that has ever happened to me.

But you can't take a plane trip away from yourself. Make yourself home, prioritize yourself, and know that *you* are everything. If I was traveling with the person I was last year, I would be feeling lost even though I am experiencing what everyone dreams of. It's an indescribable feeling the way I feel about life right now.

So, in short - yes, go travel the world if you are able to because you are going to have so many stories to tell and have so many new friends, and it will create some of the most memorable moments of your whole life. But when you get back to everyday life, prioritize your relationship with yourself.

Create your home within yourself, know that God has you, and tell your people you love them. Know no matter *what* happens to you; you are so much stronger than you think.

You can get better and love life again. It takes time, but it's so worth it. No matter where I go next, I know I will always be home. Make yourself home.

10/23/2021

Chapter 4

Letting Go of Who I Was

Dedicated to: Audrey, Jack, Dylan, Rian, Maxime, Raina,

Jack, Carolyn, Lucy, Jared, Mia, Shani, Steph, Faaris, Mattie, Noah, Daniel, Kaela

To be able to fully gain the perspective that I did, I had to let go of who I was before. It was perhaps the most important stage of my metamorphosis. Essentially, everything I ever knew about the world, I had to let go, like a caterpillar turning into a butterfly.

It was a weird feeling, honestly, like mourning a version of myself. I was still alive, but I was mourning a part of me that wasn't.

It was like looking at a different version of me, A selfish one. A part of me I wasn't proud of. But I knew this acceptance… this forgiveness for myself, was also a part of my journey.

To sit here and write about my experience in Costa Rica wouldn't do it justice. But I'll try my best. Here I was on the most beautiful, tropical land of Costa Rica. There were fifteen of us who chose Costa Rica for our community service module.

We were assigned six different non-profit organizations to devote our time to for the next six weeks. First, we went to a school where we played soccer with the kids and cleaned up their school. The next six places were mostly forest restorations, so we planted trees, mangroves, and everything in between. This made me experience nature closely, something that I never really did before.

We all knew each other from Boston. All I saw were friendly faces. I was anxious about it all, though, as I wanted to be friends with everyone. I wanted *everyone* to like me. Soon enough, I learned, why do I care if people like me? Why can't I just be *me?*

When I truly started to become my authentic self, that is when I think everything fell into place. It was identical to puzzle pieces coming together only when you realize what the original picture should have been like. I let my guard down and didn't put up any walls. So did everyone else. It was a liberating experience. One by one, we all became our true selves. It was such a surreal feeling because I got introduced to some of the greatest people ever.

I want to talk about one of the most important people in my life now, Rian. I didn't know it back then, though. A meaningful friendship that grew over the course of six weeks.

We were on the same team playing cards. She was one of my best friends in the group. I admired her so much; she made me feel like I could always count on her.

On nights when I was homesick or just a little sad, she always left the room in her bed for me to jump into. Of course, my teddy bear came with me, too. One friend out of the fifteen turned into fifteen out of fifteen - and rather quickly. In a blink of an eye, we were all telling each other our life stories. Our biggest fears, who we admire the most, our biggest dreams ... essentially: everything!

I told more things to these people within one week than I've ever told my lifelong friends and family. The conversations were endless, and it was so cool to be able to talk to them so freely, without judgment. I thought such things were unheard of, and yet they were happening to me.

We played cards every night. I thought it was so old school of us. I wasn't much into cards until I started playing. No WiFi and no cell service - not that much to do at night besides maybe having a beer and playing cards. Cards, as it turned out, became the root of our big friendship. But my group, our *tiny* little group, was safe, and so was the environment around us. You could just feel it.

We spent countless nights just laughing until we cried, losing track of all time. There were no expectations, nothing that you had to be "good enough" for, and no societal standards ... just us being in our own world, breathing the air, and helping people. I started to feel like I would do anything for these guys, and that is something I'd never felt so strongly about before. I'd never felt this kind of love.

Costa Rica forced me to come out of my comfort zone. Yeah, Europe did too, but it still had most of the basics resembling America. Huge clothing stores, thousands of different restaurants, and access to all technology.

Costa Rica, however, was a different kind of world altogether. There were no ACs, no cell phone connections, cold showers, and little space to put your things.

These factors made me become completely vulnerable and uncomfortable. I had never experienced this before; what do I do? Oh no, I didn't have access to anything at the palm of my hand in milliseconds. I didn't know what to do, but my body did. It adapted, and so did my mind. I guess that's how it must have been during the times when there wasn't any technology and when people lived in the wild and survived!

It was so crazy to me how you can adapt to change so quickly. I guess this is something all of us inherit but never truly realize. *I* had changed my habitual ways of 18 years in 2 weeks. How amazing was that?

Your mind is capable of so many things: you *just* have to push it. My mind was so pure. The only question on my mind was: should I play soccer or go to the waterfall later?

My body knew how to live so organically, yet I wanted to scroll aimlessly on Instagram. An endless loop that I broke in six weeks. What do I do when my phone doesn't have a connection? I was so ignorant. I didn't even look at what was in front of me. Nature. I myself experienced the most beautiful crystal-blue waters, breathtaking wildlife, and, most importantly, the people. I was truly blessed.

I saw a different version of people when I went to Costa Rica. Costa Ricans weren't like Americans - they didn't want anything. Not only did they not *want* anything, but they also didn't need anything - and they were still happy. It is a place of 'pura vida' or pure life. I noticed how their traditional dresses were so remarkable and full of colors.

The women wore a long and wavy skirt (or a frock) with a shoulderless blouse. It had shirred fabric around the chest. Their garb was usually full of bright colors. I learned that the men's traditional dress is pants (usually white, black, or denim) coupled with a white shirt.

They also wore a kerchief around their neck and a hat, which was brimmed and white in color, called *a chonete*. They wore a colorful belt too, which was red in color mostly. For feet, both men and women were often found wearing leather sandals. They embraced their culture, and didn't care what anyone thought.

These people chose the good life. It was visible even in their dresses, full of life. Their ability to look at situations and confront everything with their optimistic lifestyle was astonishing. It didn't matter how much money they had, what their clothes looked like, what car they drove, nothing. They would smile at you and go about their lives.

The only 3 things that they valued were family, food, and nature. The Costa Ricans truly lived so authentically, so freely. It encouraged all of us to just be who we are. I can't even explain how much I admired them; I wanted to be just like them. Every day, slowly, I tried to shift my perspective to mimic theirs.

Costa Rica also has diverse wildlife. To see animals up close was an experience too. Sloths are very common, and it is said that you can spot them yourself if you go to national parks and even forests. They usually hang around the trees and are considered lazy. I beg to differ. I feel they are just living the simple life.

I also learned about other wildlife and was able to spot them myself. Birds, for instance, I used them to remember to always keep an eye on the sky. While I wasn't always able to identify them, it was nice to see them.

I was also introduced to a place called *Territorio de Zaguates,* or Land of Stray Dogs, which, as the name suggests, is filled with stray dogs! It's like a small town where you'd find all these dogs. I had wanted to visit it but I couldn't as it was a bit far from where we were.

I actually witnessed some animals go through adaptation, change, persevere, and keep going on with their life. I saw them get uncomfortable - and then grow from it. I can't stress this enough - you need to get uncomfortable to get comfortable again.

A butterfly must break open the cocoon from the inside; that's the only way it can fly. If I had never experienced something like this, I would not have developed into the person I am today. Change your environment. You cannot grow in the place you are stuck in. Your mind *will* adapt.

You need to change your environment - even just for a little while. Break the monotony. You need to see what the world has to offer. I promise you can only benefit from it. Breaking the hamster wheel of your life is the first step.

Hopping around between six different places every week was honestly a little exhausting. It's like right when you started to get comfy, you had to pack up and leave for the next destination.

Being completely vulnerable and uncomfortable left such an emptiness that was almost calling to be filled.

Calling to be filled with laughter, with love, with ocean waves. I let go of a little part of me so I could leave room for it.

Chapter 5

The Value Of Life

Costa Rica marked a point in my life that proved to be an eye-opening experience. I had felt high on life. I didn't think anything could beat my experience there. But, as it turned out, my next destination gave Costa Rica some real competition. After an uneventful flight, I finally arrived on the Galapagos Islands.

We were all here; all 80 of us were back together. This time, it was completely different; we were comfortable. We had grown accustomed to each other; we were a family now, even though the last time I'd seen some of these people was the first two weeks backpacking around Europe. It felt like years ago at this point.

We had experienced so much in such a short timeframe that the first few weeks felt so long ago! Maybe it was just that I felt like I'd grown up so much in just a few months.

I thought when we would all come together again; I would just cling to my Costa Rica crew. But that wasn't the case. I didn't realize that the other groups also got as close as we did in Costa Rica. So when we all did reunite, we all had different perspectives on the world. We didn't disconnect from the different groups; we *merged*. We merged perfectly.

Everyone was so welcoming and willing to start over and make new friends. All the anxiety that came along with expressing yourself was thrown out the window. Why so? Because all of us individually realized that we were just going to be who we were. To be able to witness this happen, to witness everybody become their own unique self, was something right out of a movie. But it *wasn't* a movie.

My experience here was nothing short of extraordinary. The Galapagos Islands were unbelievable. No, I wish I could show you guys. It was all truly unbelievable. Hands down, it was the most breathtaking place I have ever laid my eyes on. Every detail, every piece of nature, everything was so finely crafted.

So, the Galapagos Islands are an archipelago (a collection of islands). They happen to be volcanic islands and are famous for being an inspiration for naturalist Charles Darwin, who studied different animal species there. In fact, the name Galapagos (galápagos) actually means tortoises in Spanish!

As I let the magic of this place in, I realized it was different from America in the best way. I was so free here. Soaking up the sun all day and laughing all night. When we would go out to the bar, we met people from everywhere. It was the coolest thing ever, being able to talk to new people and hear their stories.

Why they're here, who they are, where they come from, everything. You essentially learn everything about a complete stranger, become best friends for the night, and never see them again. But in the Galapagos, they always came from a cool story.

They'd tell you how they absolutely loved their life. I was amazed how they could feel so contented with how little they had. They weren't programmed to always see the bad side; they only saw the good. And when we met people from America, being at the same bar as us, it felt bizarre. Some people were actually from nearby towns, like some of my friends! How small and big the world was! We all agreed how crazy this place was.

Like how cool is it to be able to experience something like this? We would talk about it all night after having a few drinks. There was no care in the world. I also learned more about Charles Darwin.

I think I was initially introduced to him in middle school; I knew he was some guy that discovered something. But the land I was standing on was the same land that Darwin used to discover his theory, and realizing that was such an amazing feeling.

They even had a whole museum with all his history. His theory states that species can change over time, that new species come from preexisting species, and that all species share a common ancestor. It actually made me think back to Barcelona when I realized that my host family had the same values as me. These same values now apply to people in Costa Rica and the Galapagos, too.

I was starting to think maybe everyone I meet comes from the same origin. We are all the same. Some might have more money or look differently, but deep down, we all feel the same way.

I can't explain it; I just know that everyone is somehow connected. This life isn't something that just happened. We all came from the same root. I don't know what root and we all have different ideas of what that root is. However, our human experience unites us in ways that we don't even realize. We're not really strangers.

I learned that seals lived on the island, too. Similar to dogs in America, they would relax on the park bench with their bellies up. It was so funny! You'd be walking to lunch and see a seal just hanging out. Or you'd see the natives selling some sort of souvenir jewelry. They'd be smiling from ear to ear, even though no one was buying their goods.

Similar to Costa Ricans, they made enough to live and didn't need anything more. It's called the simple life. When you make enough to survive, but don't ruin your body to exhaustion. They honestly just spent most of their time by the water, not working. I smiled back at them.

We spent the next 3 weeks doing the craziest, unforgettable adventures. We hiked outrageous mountains, experienced the unique culture, and watched tiny sharks, but the most memorable of all, we snorkeled!

We snorkeled 5 different times in 3 weeks. I didn't realize that the world in the water could be more beautiful than the land. Above, the water was amazing, but underwater was something indescribable. The first time I jumped in the water, I saw multi-colored iguanas swimming next to me. I was internally freaking out because I had never seen an iguana swim, let alone swim less than a foot away from my face!

Well, apparently, the iguanas can swim; and, in fact, are harmless. There weren't only iguanas, though. Every type of fish was swimming next to me. The water was crystal clear, so you could see the face and body of every magical creature underwater.

Maybe I'd seen some pictures of these little guys or seen fish like these in movies, but nothing compared to witnessing this firsthand.

I couldn't even believe how real everything was. They had undeniable life in them. Just imagine, the same guy that created those fish created you and me; how could that be? We think of ourselves so horribly, not deserving, yet we are perfectly and intentionally handcrafted, just like these fish. These fish were beautiful, almost heavenly. I didn't realize that fish could allow me to dig deeper. Fish? How dumb. They were just fish. But after traveling, I tended to dig deeper into everything. Every single thing.

I was finally starting to think on my own, not listening to what others had to say. But the fish was the first time I realized that I was starting to think bigger. I never noticed it before. Ironic, isn't it? Such small creatures reshaping my whole perspective on life?

Now that I think about it, I was actually starting to think like Mary. It was all coming full circle. Snorkeling was it for me. It allowed me to see true wildlife face-to-face. It opened my eyes to all the unknown creations in this world.

It was groundbreaking- This world is enormous; everything has life in it. If you look into every aspect of your life, there is value in everything. But the thing is, as individuals, we choose how much value goes into each.

If you value your health, you try to eat the healthiest food. If you value your family, you make sure they know you love them. If you value your friendships, you spend quality time with them. If you value compassion, you feel deeply for other people.

I could have a neverending list of different values. But when you put all your values together, you have the value of your life. You have carefully and clearly designed your life exactly how you want. Or have you? Have you set up your life how you want?

That's okay; most people haven't. Most people strive to be what they think people want or what their parents want them to be. Or they get distracted by the short-term dopamine rushes you get these days.

You know what I'm talking about- social media, partying, video games, weed. But what's stopping you from personalizing your life? Essentially, your aligned values will create the person you are. So what is actually stopping you from being the best version of yourself? If you value health, prove it. If you value your family, show them. If you value compassion, convey it.

There is not enough time to half-say and half-do things. If you're going to say something, say it. And if you want to do something, then do it.

Don't waste your life. There is only a short list of values you need to be fulfilled. You can wipe your soul clean. I did. Start over, stand back, and look at your life from a higher view. Figure out your values, and worship them. Be obsessed with them. Your values create who you are. The value of life is so gentle, so precious. It can be ripped from you at any given second. So don't take it for granted; align your values and realize what is truly important.

I soaked up every day and every moment. My time spent here was full of love, light, and life. I knew there was no way I would experience something like this ever again. This is the place where my soul and values align.

Chapter 6

On My Own

I was on my own now.

Not literally, but close to it. I was given an internship in Stockholm, Sweden. It was a part of the program. You choose your destination, and your advisor assigns you an internship based on your interests. This was going to be the next chapter in my journey. I was so grateful to be here. I was just about coming out of my cocoon. Being on my own was the most crucial part of my metamorphosis.

When we landed, our advisor met us on the ground. We drove to our new place. We were all so excited. There were about 10 of us here. We were going to be living on our own now. Scary but exciting. None of us have ever lived alone before.

We were only kids, fresh out of high school, with a whole world in front of us. The staff handed us our keys and gave us our room numbers. Thankfully, Rian's room was literally two steps down the hall. I unlocked the door and stepped into the room. It was beautiful, luxurious, and everything I ever needed. A kitchen, bathroom, table, and bed - all the essentials. It wasn't huge; it was just the perfect size.

For the next thirty minutes, I did something I'd never done before. I honestly thought it was kind of weird and was wondering how I even thought of it. I wrote down a list of things that have molded me into who I am today. The things I was so grateful for. A very simple but strange question, no? How often does one think about it?

When I started jotting the things down, they ranged from my best friends and my old dog to traveling and classmates from elementary school - I wrote down just about everything I could think of.

By the time I was finished, I had counted about 100 things. Then I thought of some more and added 20. I looked down at the paper, then looked around at my tiny home for the next 6 weeks. Everything that has ever happened to me and everyone that has been in my life has allowed me to be in this moment right now.

I jumped on my bed just like I would as a little kid. It felt like my life had come full circle. I felt like a grown-up, but internally, I was still that little girl that had no care in the world. I felt like I was becoming her again.

I finally got up, ready to make my place cozy. I started unpacking all my clothes and putting them into my spacious closet. I realized I needed to go to the store because I had clothes suitable for the tropical Galapagos Islands, not for the frigid cold in Sweden!

I honestly didn't know how to shop for myself, either. My mom would buy me clothes, or I'd go with her to get them. I'd never been in a foreign country trying to navigate a new city to buy some winter clothes. Our first night here was actually the Super Bowl. It made me think of my friends at home. My friends and I would always watch the Super Bowl together. But I was here now, and they were at college. We were growing up.

I remember it was the biggest struggle trying to live stream the game since they didn't televise it in Europe. I really wanted to cook something for my friends, you know, to celebrate our next step. I was also just so excited to cook on my new stove.

I don't know why; it just felt so exciting. The supermarket was right across from our apartment, so it was only a two-minute walk. It was honestly the first time I bought groceries by myself too.

I grabbed pasta, milk, cheese, salt, and pepper. I was going to make the Mac and Cheese I always made at home. I almost about set the whole building on fire during the process, but I perfected the recipe and proudly walked down the hall with my famous Mac and Cheese in hand.

It reminded me of home. I was greeted by about eight of my friends in a room suitable for one. That first night was entertaining and comforting, to say the least. It set the tone of independence for the next six weeks. Just like Barcelona and Costa Rica, I knew these six weeks would fly by. I made sure to get the most out of this time.

My internship had begun. Remember the kid I fell asleep with on our first flight to Paris? He was also in Stockholm and had the same internship as me. He also became a really good friend of mine throughout the next couple of weeks.

Our internship was with a financial company called Fairlo. I was kind of disappointed because I'm not really into finances, so I didn't think I would like it that much. But I kept my hopes up and was just grateful to be given an internship. It took us so long to get there on our first day because we had no idea how to use the trams since everything was in Swedish!

Once we had finally arrived, I remember being nervous; I wanted to make a good impression and be professional. I've never had to act that way before, so this was uncharted territory for me. We walked up the stairs and laughed because we had no idea if we should shake their hands or hug them. I felt like a real adult like I was stepping into the real world.

I don't know why so many people say "the real world," like I never really understood what it meant. For me, it just meant the eye-opening step from the innocence you perceive to eventually seeing the harsh reality of the world.

The first steps that I took into the office felt welcoming. Everyone who walked by smiled or gestured. The bosses came over to us with open arms and smiling faces; they were so welcoming. Thank goodness they initiated it first because we never figured out how we should greet them!

They were two women. I don't know why, but I just thought it would be men because that's how it usually is. I learned later that women don't play a lesser role than men in the workplace, like in America. They actually play a huge role in businesses in Sweden.

It made me feel hopeful that maybe I could run a business someday. And they weren't typically mean bosses; they were soft-spoken. They were kind and understanding, and so were their employees. You could see how you become what you are surrounded by.

Getting to know the ground rules and layout of the company was unreal to me. They got to come in on their own time, almost like the company revolved around the employees, not the bosses. They took paid sick days, mental health days, maternity days, or days they didn't feel like coming in. I couldn't believe it. Then I felt stupid that

I thought it was crazy that a human cared about another human to give them the time they needed. Isn't that how it should be? They weren't just there to work like machines and then go home. The bosses valued their workers; they understood the human part of 'human resources.'

And in the long run, it is better for the whole company. You have happy employees who could last a long time, with excellent efficiency.

We all entered a room, and it took 30 minutes for the bosses to learn about who we were and our interests. After they learned that we both liked working out, they bought us a monthly gym membership. They also discussed our role in the company. We just had to take pictures of the city for them to put on their website. They didn't want to stick us in an office all day; they wanted us to explore the city. I was so grateful to be able to be a part of this.

The next couple of weeks were critical for me. It was the key to my development. Being alone. From a young age, we're taught that we need relationships to live. Don't get me wrong; I genuinely do believe that that's the biggest blessing in life. But you don't need it to survive.

You're born alone, and you die alone. You don't need anybody. Your heart can beat on its own, your mind can think on its own, and your body can move on its own. Stop selling yourself short. You are capable of doing *anything* alone. However, being alone was completely foreign to me. Actually, it was non-existent in my 18 years of life.

I had lived in an eight-person household and always had many friends by my side. It's not that I didn't love that, but it's just that I didn't know who I was without them. I was never alone because I had the best friends and family ever. But *here* I was, alone.

It's not that I was alone all the time, though. I did go to work and clubs, hung out with Rian in her room, drank at the bars, and went to the gym - I did a lot. But the majority of my time was spent alone, and at first, it was kind of uncomfortable.

For instance, once, I hadn't spoken to anyone all day, so I whispered "Hello" in my room, just so I made sure my voice was still there. I also found myself having a few rough nights when I had to sleep in Rian's room. But soon enough, the uncomfortable feeling turned liberating.

The biggest thing I learned while being in Stockholm was not through going out to all the clubs and cafes, traveling to Amsterdam and other cities... It was learning how to be by myself. In the next six weeks, I fell in love with myself.

That might sound so weird, but it was true. Maybe not in love, but being so content with being alone that I didn't need anybody else. The little flaws I examined, the imperfections, started to disappear little by little. In a short amount of time, I learned that the only person you will have for the rest of your life is you.

You are everything. It takes a very long time for people to accept that. But it was almost overnight for me.

Traveling had brought me to this point of grace, this point of peace with myself. It allowed me to become whoever I wanted. The layout and the way that I experienced this year was perfect. Being on my own for my last destination was like when you finally find the last piece of the puzzle. Or when a butterfly takes its first flight out of the cocoon.

It allowed me to reflect and learn how to survive on my own. I couldn't depend on anyone else. Every mistake was mine, mostly because no one else was to blame. That was the best day of my life; the day I decided my life was my own. No apologies and no excuses. No one to lean on, rely on, or put the blame on. This was the day my life truly began, and this was the first time I had truly realized it.

I finally came to the knowledge that everything on this earth is attainable - if you want it. And I wanted it. I didn't want life to pass me by. I wanted to live. If you don't carry that pride within yourself, you will never achieve anything. You are your biggest enthusiast, your biggest admirer. Why wouldn't you be? You know that you will be with yourself 100% of your life.

If you really need somebody else to complete you, to fill you up entirely, you are in trouble. You will never become the person you were meant to be. The only person that completes you is yourself. It just might take you a while to realize it.

So, slow down and take your time. Take the time to learn about yourself - learn about the world. You will figure it out along the way. The moment you realize that you are enough, that you are something so special. That your spark is so unique and can never be taken away from you. Once you realize that, you won't consider what anyone thinks of you. You won't even care. Because between then and now, you became invested in who you were. Not who everybody tells you to be. Not *how* everybody wants you to act. You are destroying yourself if you let somebody dictate who you are. Don't let other people tell you who you are. That is one of the biggest mistakes you could ever make.

As Howard Thurman said, "There is something in every one of you that waits and listens for the sound of the genuine in yourself. It is the only true guide you will ever have. And if you cannot hear it, you will all of your life spend your days on the ends of strings that somebody else pulls."

To my surprise, living alone turned out to be the most rewarding part of my journey. It showed me what I was capable of and what I thought I was never capable of.

Chapter 7

Home

Saying goodbye to the people who collectively changed everything for me was one of the hardest things I've ever had to do. Every single person in my gap year, the strangers that turned into best friends, implanted something of their own inside of me. This includes even the strangers I met at the bar for a couple of hours!

Whether it was the way they said a certain word, how they treated other people, the jokes they made, how often they called their family, the way they ate - just everything. I picked up on everything, every little detail.

We all adored each other, so when we all went our separate ways, we carried a piece of each other within us. That still lives on when I call them today, and they constantly use my favorite word. It's amazing to me how we are all reflections of the people we love. I was *home* now. It was so good to be here.

The home was safe; the home was vulnerable. It felt like I was in a movie where the girl returned to her hometown. But it obviously wasn't that deep.

However, it was the most fantastic feeling to be reunited with my family and best friends. It was bittersweet, though. Leaving behind a turning point in my life but continuing on in my story. I kept every single moment in me, through me.

Every person, place, and memory I made along the way radiated through me in everyday life. Which I am forever grateful for.

People always told me that once you go to college, and when you finally return home, it will never be the same as it was. And I saw so much more than a small college town, so I think it hit me a little harder than most. It's weird because you could picture your hometown; the local coffee shops, high school football fields, the grocery stores. And when you return home, you still see those places. But it's different. It really doesn't feel the same.

You're trying to remember how it used to be, but it's just nostalgia, *not* the present. It doesn't feel like senior year spring break in the car with your friends, windows down, and music blasting. I don't know the best way to explain it - but if you, too, have felt like this, I'm sure you understand. The home you felt in high school isn't the same.

Why? It's literally the same place - but it feels so different. How am I supposed to live a normal life after seeing what I saw? It was such a weird feeling. A feeling that was a bit overwhelming for me. I knew I had to accept it, or I couldn't move past it. I also got so many concerns (from people who barely knew me) when I returned home.

"I hope you had an amazing time. Now you have to work the rest of your life."

"You'll never be able to go back to school after this past year."

"You'll never experience happiness like that again!"

Why are people like that? Constantly dimming the light, constantly shrinking their mind to society's standards, and constantly dictating other people's lives. It's so weird.

And it's always from people who don't know anything about you, the people who hate their lives so much that they project it on others. People who have never been in your shoes. It's like, how about you run your life, and I'll run mine.

If you want to know a big piece of truth, things people say to you are usually a judgment of themselves. How somebody speaks to you or how somebody treats you is almost always a direct reflection of themselves. Just remember that. But I didn't love talking about my experience this past year. To me, it felt like I was bragging.

I knew how incredible my year was, so I always tried to keep it to myself. It was something spiritual that I felt should echo within me. That's why I started writing.

I never really loved writing at all, but maybe that's because it was always long research essays I was forced to complete in school. I realized my mind wandered differently when I wrote about something I was passionate about.

But this one question I got will always stick with me. It was, "Has traveling shifted your perspective on the world?" It took me a couple of seconds to think about it, but when I got the words together, I said something like this: when I think about something shifting, I imagine the shift to be a little change in the right direction.

But for me, my shift was drastic. I didn't really know who I was before I started traveling. I was wrapped up in my own world, thinking I was defined by my problems. In fact, I was defined by what everyone told me to be.

I never thought for myself, but I never even had the opportunity to. I was just a kid listening to what everyone told me. I was living so structurally, but so was everyone around me. However, nobody seemed to care for some reason. They went through the same motions every day. Nobody was dying to seek more in life; they just complained and complained but never actually took the step to change.

Traveling lets you learn about yourself in ways you wouldn't believe; it lets you grow into who you want to be. Traveling has 100% shifted my perspective on the world. It allowed me to think broader, love harder, seek more, and, most importantly, travel more. Being healthy and able to travel the world is one of the biggest blessings I have ever received.

Little by little, I started to put my whole self into everything. I had an internal peace, an internal happiness that couldn't stop shining. It felt so bright, so magical. It was similar to the feeling I felt before I decided to take the gap year. The internal ball was on fire. But this time, it didn't feel like it was consuming me; it was actually radiating me. The void I had been seeking has been fulfilled. I wanted everyone to experience what I did.

Not just traveling but just getting the most out of your life. To not settle for the life that you don't want. But why wouldn't you? To me, it seemed so blatantly obvious that if you don't like something, leave. And if you want something, go for it. I don't know if it was just me, but it just seemed so simple.

I didn't understand why people were so scared of taking that jump, being different, and doing something most people didn't. It was so clear to me. I guess I just had that uniqueness in me ever since I was a little kid. It never really bothered me to be different. It actually never even occurred to me.

I thought more about young people and how the desire to travel more and escape the 9-5 mentality is growing rapidly every day. I think that many young adults who want to take a leap and follow their passions are fearful of what society will say. I picture society as a box. Society has been created to fit in a box.

If you step out of the box, you are not normal. The judgment and embarrassment that comes with stepping out of the box is enough for people not to step out of the box entirely. But people don't know that stepping out of the box will actually open up countless opportunities and doors.

It will allow you to think bigger, smarter, and deeper. Traveling opens your eyes and heart to what the world has to offer. It will grow you as a person, a more insightful person.

So if I had to talk to the young people that want to live the "unconventional lifestyle" and see more of the world, it is to just do it. Take the leap of faith. You will never put out the fire that is passionately burning inside of you unless you do it. There is no such thing as a "traditional lifestyle." You get to create the life you want.

Don't jeopardize it because you fear you won't fit in the box. Something that put this into perspective for me was Googling an image of the universe. We are nothing compared to this immeasurable place. Recognizing the entirety of the universe is something so difficult to grasp. Realize that your mind is its own universe, too.

Your energy is the same energy that consumes the entire solar system. So keep your eyes on the stars and your feet on the ground because you have a whole universe inside you: the energy that you have created. And it fits perfectly in the universe. It actually wouldn't be complete without it.

Coming from someone who had no idea who she was two years ago, I want you to know that it is never too late to change your life. Once you start seeing the beauty in this life, the darkness starts disappearing. It doesn't matter if you're 85 or 15; the day you become free and truly start living will be the pivotal point in your life. And when it happens, you'll know what I'm talking about.

The lessons that I have learned in one year are indescribable, and no amount of words will do them justice.

But, if I had to give you one last piece of encouragement: I truly hope that you take the leap and go after whatever fire ignites in you. The world is waiting for you.

I actually think about the world like a book. God has given you an entire book to read, explore, and to learn from. For those who don't travel, only stay on the first page.

But how will you live if you forever stay on the first page? You don't want to be the person that never got to see the world, and who the world never got the chance to see.

Made in United States
North Haven, CT
02 April 2023